A TRUE BOOK™

Extreme Science Careers

ANN O. SQUIRE

Children's Press®
An Imprint of Scholastic Inc.
New York Toronto London Auckland Sydney
Mexico City New Delhi Hong Kong
Danbury, Connecticut

Content Editor
Robert Wolffe, EdD
Professor
Bradley University, Peoria, Illinois

Library of Congress Cataloging-in-Publication Data
Squire, Ann, author.
 Extreme science careers / by Ann O. Squire.
   pages cm. — (A true book)
 Audience: 9–12.
 Audience: Grade 4 to 6.
 Includes bibliographical references and index.
 ISBN 978-0-531-20744-4 (lib. bdg. : alk. paper) — ISBN 978-0-531-21555-5 (pbk. : alk. paper)
 1. Science—Vocational guidance—Juvenile literature. 2. Scientists—Juvenile literature. I. Title.
 Q147.S68 2015
 502.3—dc23   2014005457

All rights reserved. Published in 2015 by Children's Press, an imprint of Scholastic Inc.
Printed in China 62
SCHOLASTIC, CHILDREN'S PRESS, A TRUE BOOK™, and associated logos are trademarks and/or registered trademarks of Scholastic Inc.

1 2 3 4 5 6 7 8 9 10 R 24 23 22 21 20 19 18 17 16 15

Front cover: Scientists Maurice and Katia Krafft film the Piton de la Fournaise volcano
Back cover: Researcher holding flask

Find the Truth!

Everything you are about to read is true *except* for one of the sentences on this page.

Which one is **TRUE**?

T or F   Scientists regularly fly through the centers of hurricanes.

T or F   No one has ever visited the deepest known place in Earth's oceans.

Find the answers in this book.

Contents

1 Extreme Scientists

Where do some extreme scientists work? 7

2 Exploring Earth

How do researchers explore a cave
filled with water? 11

3 Up in the Air

What do Hurricane Hunters find in a
hurricane's eye? 19

THE BIG TRUTH!

Marie Curie

What kind of scientific research cost
Curie her life? 26

**Marie Curie in her
laboratory**

4

DeepSea diving submersible

4 Working in the Water

How did 19th-century scientists measure the depth of the ocean? 29

5 The Ends of the Earth

Why are researchers isolated during the winter at the South Pole? 37

True Statistics 44

Resources 45

Important Words 46

Index 47

About the Author 48

Rain forests contain more than half of Earth's plant and animal species.

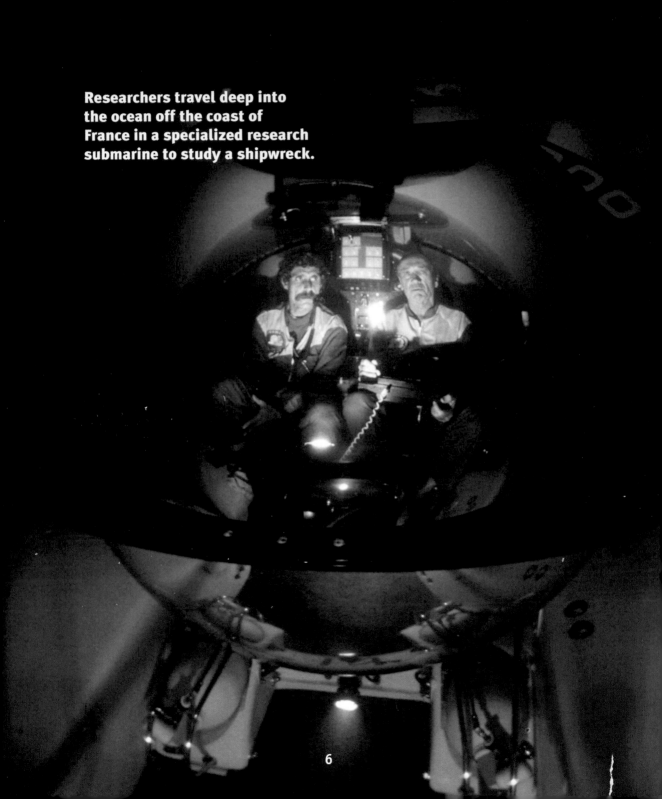

Researchers travel deep into the ocean off the coast of France in a specialized research submarine to study a shipwreck.

CHAPTER 1

Extreme Scientists

Extreme science careers can take researchers far from their comfort zone. Some researchers travel to places where working—even staying alive—is a challenge. The inside of a volcano, the **eye** of a hurricane, the bottom of the ocean, and the middle of a rain forest are just a few places you'll find extreme scientists. After you meet these daring researchers, you'll never look at science in the same way again.

Research submarines use powerful lights to brighten the dark ocean floor.

In the Lab

Do you ever wonder what it would be like to be a scientist? Do you imagine yourself in a huge lab full of test tubes and gadgets? Many brilliant researchers work in laboratories. Some try to discover the secrets of dangerous—sometimes deadly—**elements**. Others spend a cold, isolated winter at a South Pole lab to study the Antarctic ice fields.

Some research buildings are small and simple, such as this one on Ross Island in Antarctica.

A "storm chaser" jumps out of a research truck as a storm brews in Nebraska.

In the Field

Do you picture yourself in the field instead of in a lab? Do you dream of chasing after massive storms? Maybe you see yourself sliding down a rope into the deepest parts of the earth. Many people think of science as difficult, dull, and boring. They don't realize that science careers can be full of adventure and excitement.

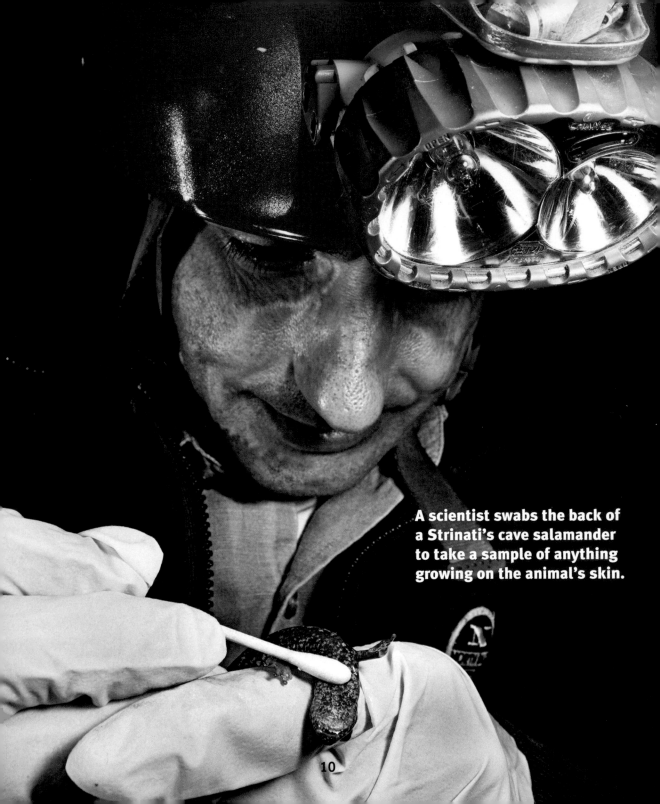

A scientist swabs the back of a Strinati's cave salamander to take a sample of anything growing on the animal's skin.

CHAPTER 2

Exploring Earth

For some extreme scientists, there is no better subject to study than our own planet. Speleologists (spee-lee-AH-luh-jists) explore Earth's nooks and crannies. They study how caves form and the types of life-forms that survive in them. Seismologists focus on earthquakes and other sources of underground vibration. Volcanologists specialize in volcanoes, especially ones that are active.

 Strinati's cave salamanders were not discovered until 1958.

In some caves, ice is present all year round. These are called ice caves.

Speleologist at Work

Italian speleologist Giovanni Badino has traveled all over the world to study caves. Nepal, Chile, Iceland, and Antarctica are just a few of the places he has visited. Badino is especially interested in the climate inside caves. A cave's climate is much more stable than the climate in the outside world. A small change in temperature or humidity inside a cave can have a major effect. These changes leave long-lasting clues etched into the cave's walls.

Underground Dangers

Being a cave researcher is not easy. The first hurdle is getting inside the cave. In Europe, many cave entrances are vertical. In these cases, speleologists use methods similar to those practiced by mountain climbers. To enter, they lower themselves into a cave using ropes. Once inside, they find an environment that is dark, damp, and cold. Dripping water, slippery floors, and loose rocks add to the hazards every cave scientist faces.

Speleologists sometimes have to hoist themselves up just to reach a cave's entrance.

Cave Diving

Other caves are filled with water. Researchers must use **scuba diving** equipment to move through the cave. Considering the difficulty and the dangers, it is not surprising that cave research is not one of the more popular science careers. But caves can tell us a lot about the history of Earth's climate and geography. Badino says that doing research inside a cave is like being the first person to study a new planet.

Divers need special training before entering underwater caves.

14

Mount Etna has been active for an estimated 2.6 million years.

An Explosive Career

Imagine standing on the edge of an active volcano. You peer down into a steaming, lava-filled crater. Volcanology is the study of volcanoes and volcanic eruptions. It is an exciting and extreme career, but it does not have to be dangerous. Most volcanologists plan their expeditions carefully, focusing on safety first. "No measurement is worth your life," says Tamsin Mather. Mather is a volcanologist who has studied volcanoes in Nicaragua, Chile, and Italy.

Special tools allow researchers to take samples of volcanic gases to study back at a lab.

Mather studies the plumes of gas that rise from some active volcanoes. The plumes may contain dangerous chemicals, so she wears a gas mask for protection. In addition to toxic fumes, Mather and her team cope with exhausting climbs to the summit of a volcano. They must carefully plan every trip up a mountain. If their computer crashes or they forget an important piece of equipment, they can't just run home for a replacement!

There are many other aspects of volcanoes to study besides plumes. These include examining the rocks and lava that may be thrown from active volcanoes. Scientists also study earthquakes, which sometimes signal a coming volcanic eruption. Another important job is predicting eruptions. For example, volcanologists successfully predicted an eruption of Mount Pinatubo in the Philippines in 1991. The prediction gave residents time to **evacuate** their homes. Thousands of lives were saved.

The cloud of dust and gases erupt from Mount Pinatubo in 1991.

A lot can be learned by studying extreme storms, such as tornadoes, up close.

18

Up in the Air

Some extreme scientists look at what goes on beneath the earth's surface. Others have their eyes on the clouds. Meteorologists are scientists who study and predict weather. Violent weather, such as hurricanes and tornadoes, can cause massive damage and destruction. When a storm is forming, meteorologists learn as much as they can about it. This helps them make predictions and issue warnings that could save the lives of people in the storm's path.

Tornadoes were photographed for the first time in the 1880s.

Hurricane Hunters

It is tough to gather information about a storm if you are not close to it. So some meteorologists study storms in the most extreme way possible: by flying directly into them! The Air Force Reserve's Weather Reconnaissance Squadron has been braving the high winds of hurricanes since 1944. These Hurricane Hunters use large, heavy airplanes that can carry more than 40,000 pounds (18,144 kilograms) of crew members and equipment.

This photo shows the view from inside a weather reconnaissance plane.

Hurricane Hunters collect data as often as once a minute during a mission.

The National Hurricane Center in Miami, Florida, looks for areas of bad weather that might become a hurricane. When they find one, they send the Hurricane Hunters to investigate. The giant airplane takes off with a crew that includes a pilot, copilot, navigator, and weather officer. As the plane approaches the storm, the clouds thicken. The sky becomes dark. The crew uses the plane's weather instruments to keep track of the wind speed, temperature, and other conditions.

Sometimes a hurricane's eye is clearly defined and easy to spot at the center of the storm.

Into the Eye

The inner edge of a hurricane is a doughnut-shaped ring of thunderstorms called the eye wall. Winds in the eye wall can reach speeds of more than 150 miles (241 kilometers) per hour. They toss the plane around like a toy. Once the plane enters the storm's eye, the air is calm and clear. Although a ring of dark clouds surrounds the eye, the sky above is blue. Below, the storm kicks up huge ocean waves.

Inside the eye, the crew launches an instrument called a **dropsonde**. A mini-parachute pops out, and the dropsonde drifts toward the ocean. Along the way, it measures wind speed, temperature, humidity, and air pressure. These readings are sent back to scientists on the plane. After passing through the eye and the eye wall on the other side, the plane turns and heads back into the storm.

A Hurricane Hunters crew member loads a dropsonde to be released into a hurricane.

Hurricane Forecasts

A flight into a hurricane usually lasts around 11 hours. The plane makes several passes through the eye of the storm. With each pass, the crew launches another dropsonde. All of the data collected is sent to the National Hurricane Center (NHC). NHC computers create up-to-the-minute forecasts of the storm's strength and direction. Thanks to the Hurricane Hunters scientists, storm forecasting has greatly improved. This gives people more time to get out of the storm's path.

Meteorologists track hurricane data at the National Hurricane Center in Miami, Florida.

Extreme Science, Extreme Risks

Extreme science careers are exciting, but they can turn deadly. In 2013, "storm chaser" Tim Samaras was tracking a huge tornado over the plains of Oklahoma. His job was to place science **probes** in the tornado's path. That meant putting himself in the tornado's path. Samaras had been chasing tornadoes for many years. But on May 31, 2013, disaster struck. He and two members of his research team were killed as the tornado swept past.

Tim Samaras looks up at a stormy sky in 2005.

Marie Curie

Some scientists are extreme because of what they study and the obstacles they overcome to do the work they love. Marie Sklodowska was born in Poland in 1867. She did well in school and wanted to go to college. However, that was not possible for women in Poland at that time. Marie was determined. After helping her sister through school, she moved to France and entered a university.

She earned her degree in physics. She also met and married Pierre Curie, another scientist. Together they began to study invisible rays given off by elements like uranium. The Curies discovered two new, similar elements. The couple created the term radioactive to describe them. Marie Curie won the Nobel Prize twice for her work, once in 1903 and again in 1911. She was the first woman ever to win this prize, and the first person to win it more than once.

During World War I (1914–1918), Marie Curie learned that X-rays could be used in treating wounded soldiers. But there was a shortage of X-ray machines. She came up with the idea of moving them around on trucks. She also trained people to operate the machines.

Marie Curie died in 1934 from a blood disease caused by her exposure to radiation. She was truly a scientist who gave her life for her work.

Working in the Water

Some extreme scientists can be found in the oceans, rivers, and lakes that cover our planet. Rachel Graham is a conservation biologist whose work takes her face-to-face with whale sharks. These giants can grow to be 60 feet (18 meters) long. Graham's work is focused on protecting whale sharks and other shark species. These animals are threatened with **extinction** because of over fishing.

 Whale sharks are the largest living species of fish in the world.

Even a small shark might require a team of researchers to tag it.

Tagging Sharks

On a typical day, Graham can be found scuba diving in the waters off Belize, a country in Central America. She attaches special tags to sharks so their movements can be tracked and recorded. Learning about the sharks' habits and behaviors helps her create plans to protect them. Graham says that swimming with sharks doesn't frighten her. In fact, she sometimes feels more threatened by the shark fishermen who don't agree with her goal of protecting these animals.

Extreme Science, Extreme Risks

Extreme science careers are exciting, but they can turn deadly. In 2013, "storm chaser" Tim Samaras was tracking a huge tornado over the plains of Oklahoma. His job was to place science **probes** in the tornado's path. That meant putting himself in the tornado's path. Samaras had been chasing tornadoes for many years. But on May 31, 2013, disaster struck. He and two members of his research team were killed as the tornado swept past.

Tim Samaras looks up at a stormy sky in 2005.

Marie Curie

Some scientists are extreme because of what they study and the obstacles they overcome to do the work they love. Marie Sklodowska was born in Poland in 1867. She did well in school and wanted to go to college. However, that was not possible for women in Poland at that time. Marie was determined. After helping her sister through school, she moved to France and entered a university.

She earned her degree in physics. She also met and married Pierre Curie, another scientist. Together they began to study invisible rays given off by elements like uranium. The Curies discovered two new, similar elements. The couple created the term radioactive to describe them. Marie Curie won the Nobel Prize twice for her work, once in 1903 and again in 1911. She was the first woman ever to win this prize, and the first person to win it more than once.

During World War I (1914–1918), Marie Curie learned that X-rays could be used in treating wounded soldiers. But there was a shortage of X-ray machines. She came up with the idea of moving them around on trucks. She also trained people to operate the machines.

Marie Curie died in 1934 from a blood disease caused by her exposure to radiation. She was truly a scientist who gave her life for her work.

Exploring the Deep Sea

Some scientists are fascinated by what goes on far below the surface of the ocean. Oceans cover two-thirds of our planet's surface. They contain about 190 times as much living space as all of Earth's other environments put together. The average depth of the oceans is 2.5 miles (4 km). The deepest point yet discovered is 7 miles (11.3 km) deep. Clearly, scientists who want to study the ocean floor face some real challenges.

Compared to the size of their bodies, fangtooths have the largest teeth of any marine animal.

Many deep-sea fish, such as the fangtooth, have long, skinny fangs and large mouths.

Ocean Exploration

In 1872, a group of scientists set sail from England on a converted warship named *Challenger*. Their goal was to explore the seas. They estimated ocean depth by lowering a weight attached to a long cable into the water. Using this technique, *Challenger* scientists discovered one of the deepest areas of the ocean: the Mariana Trench. During their four-year expedition, the researchers also discovered 4,700 new plant and animal species.

Sailors and scientists aboard the *Challenger* look at new samples of ocean life.

32

Submersibles are equipped with lights, so researchers can see around them deep in the ocean.

Getting to the Bottom

The deep ocean experiences extreme pressure because of the weight of all the water above. For a long time, this limited how deep researchers could travel. These days, people explore the deepest parts of the ocean directly using small, submarine-like underwater vessels. Dr. Lisa Levin is a deepwater **oceanographer**. Levin studies ocean areas that contain less oxygen and marine life than waters near the surface. She is interested in protecting these deep ocean regions.

Alvin is only 23 feet (7 m) long.

←

Alvin

Alvin was the first **submersible** capable of taking researchers for a firsthand look at the world beneath the ocean's surface. Since 1964, *Alvin* has made more than 4,600 dives and carried 13,000 people to the seafloor. Pat Hickey is an expedition leader on the *Alvin*. He has taken the submersible on hundreds of dives to the ocean bottom. Hickey says that knowing physics, geology, chemistry, and biology all help him in his job.

James Cameron and the *Deepsea Challenger*

In 2012, explorer and filmmaker James Cameron touched down at the bottom of Challenger Deep. This is the deepest point known on Earth. Cameron piloted a specially built submersible craft called *Deepsea Challenger*. He descended a record 35,787 feet (10,908 m) below sea level. Cameron used a vacuum sampler called a slurp gun to collect small animals and **sediment**. He also used a video imaging system to capture 3-D pictures of the scene there.

James Cameron took the *Deepsea Challenger* on a brief tour of the United States before donating it to Woods Hole Oceanographic Institution in 2013.

Scientists help construct a
telescope at the Amundsen-Scott
South Pole Station.

The Ends of the Earth

At the southernmost tip of Earth is the Amundsen-Scott South Pole Station. The scientific station is built on top of a glacier. It sits 9,300 feet (2,835 m) above sea level and only a few hundred feet from the South Pole. In the winter, the weather is bitterly cold. In the summer, it is not much warmer. Scientists come from around the world to do research in astronomy, meteorology, glacier science, and other fields.

Seasons in the southern half of Earth are the opposite of those in the northern half.

Life at the South Pole

Scientists arriving at the South Pole station must be prepared for truly extreme conditions. The cold is the first thing everyone notices. In winter, the average air temperature is −76 degrees Fahrenheit (−60 degrees Celsius). The summer is warmer, but it is still really cold. The average summer temperature is only −18°F (−28°C). Researchers must limit their time outdoors because of the danger of frostbite.

Timeline of Extreme Scientists

1872
Scientists set sail on a voyage to explore the world's oceans aboard the *Challenger*.

1903
Marie Curie wins her first Nobel Prize.

Summer and Winter

During the summer, about 200 people live and work at the station. That number drops to about 50 during the winter. Because the station is so far south, the sun rises and sets only twice each year. It comes up in September and sets in March. For summer visitors, this means six months of continuous daylight. This may be strange, but it doesn't compare to the six months of darkness that winter residents endure.

1991
Volcanologists predict the eruption of Mount Pinatubo, saving thousands of lives.

1944
The Air Force Reserve's Weather Reconnaissance Squadron is created.

2012
James Cameron explores the bottom of Challenger Deep in a submersible craft.

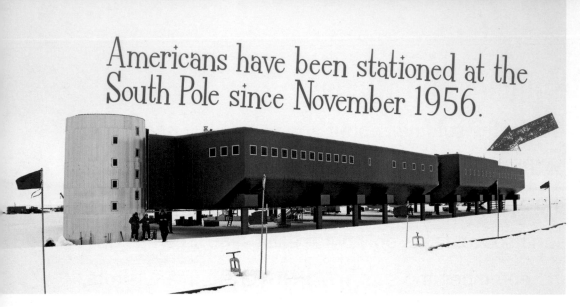

Americans have been stationed at the South Pole since November 1956.

A group of researchers stands outside the Amundsen-Scott station.

Winter Isolation

Scientists who choose to remain at the Amundsen-Scott station during the winter are completely isolated. The darkness, cold, and gale-force winds make it impossible for airplanes to fly in or out. Food, medical supplies, fuel, and other necessities must all be brought in before winter starts. Winter residents, called winter-overs, get used to dealing with everything from daily tasks to serious medical emergencies on their own.

Rain Forest Research

Researchers deep in the rain forests of South America may enjoy warm weather, but they have their own difficulties to face. The first is getting there. **Ecologist** Emilio Bruna starts with an overnight flight to Brazil. This is followed by several shorter flights to the country's interior. Then comes a long trip by truck to a remote camp. There, Bruna spends weeks at a time studying tropical plants, animals, and their relationships.

Members of an expedition into the rain forests of Papua, New Guinea, set up camp.

In the rain forest, Bruna and his team deal with hot, humid weather. They also face mosquitoes, snakes, and other dangerous animals. There's a constant risk of contracting tropical diseases such as dengue fever or malaria.

For Bruna, the risks are worth it. He says, "I can't envision myself doing anything else." It's a safe bet that most other extreme scientists feel exactly the same way. ★

A researcher takes a closer look at a specimen in Rwanda.

How to Become an Extreme Scientist

If you are taking science classes and doing experiments in school, you're already on your way to becoming a scientist. It is important to do well in science. Math and writing are also important. These will help you analyze and write about your experiments' results.

After high school, you will probably need four years of college. You may also need some additional training in your field. It takes a lot of effort. But if you are like many extreme scientists, you'll be so interested in your topic that the work will feel more like play.

True Statistics

Number of volcanic eruptions around the world each year: 50 to 70

Number of volcanic eruptions in the past 10,000 years: 1,300 to 1,500

Average size of a hurricane's eye: 20 to 40 mi. (32 to 64 km) across

Average number of hurricanes that develop over the Atlantic Ocean, Caribbean Sea, or Gulf of Mexico each year: 10

Lowest temperature ever recorded at the Amundsen-Scott South Pole Station: −117.0°F (−82.8°C), set on June 23, 1982

Highest temperature ever recorded at the Amundsen-Scott South Pole Station: 9.9°F (−12.3°C), set on December 25, 2011

Did you find the truth?

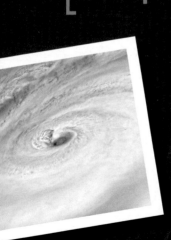

T Scientists regularly fly through the centers of hurricanes.

F No one has ever visited the deepest known place in Earth's oceans.

Resources

Books

Britton, Arthur K. *Life at a Polar Research Station*. New York: Gareth Stevens Publishing, 2013.

Rusch, Elizabeth. *Eruption! Volcanoes and the Science of Saving Lives*. New York: Houghton Mifflin Harcourt, 2013.

Treaster, Joseph B. *Hurricane Force: In the Path of America's Deadliest Storms*. New York: Kingfisher, 2007.

Visit this Scholastic Web site for more information on extreme science careers:
★ www.factsfornow.scholastic.com
Enter the keywords **Extreme Science Careers**

Important Words

dropsonde (DRUHP-suhnd) — a data-gathering instrument that is attached to a parachute and released from an airplane

ecologist (i-KAH-luh-jist) — a person who studies the relationships between living things and their environment

elements (EL-uh-muhnts) — substances that cannot be divided up into simpler substances

evacuate (i-VAK-yoo-ate) — to move away from an area or building because it is dangerous there

extinction (ik-STINK-shuhn) — the state of no longer being found alive

eye (EYE) — the calm, clear area at the center of a hurricane

oceanographer (oh-shuh-NAH-gruh-fur) — a person who studies the ocean and the plants and animals that live in it

probes (PROHBZ) — tools or devices used to explore or examine something

radioactive (ray-dee-oh-AK-tiv) — made up of atoms whose nuclei break down, giving off harmful particles

scuba diving (SKOO-buh DYE-ving) — underwater swimming with a tank of air on the swimmer's back that can be breathed through a hose

sediment (SED-uh-muhnt) — material that settles at the bottom of a liquid, such as the ocean

submersible (suhb-MUR-suh-bul) — a usually small underwater craft used especially for deep-sea research

Index

Page numbers in **bold** indicate illustrations

airplanes, **20**, 21, 22, **23**, 24, **39**, 40
Alvin (submersible), 34
Amundsen-Scott South Pole Station, **36**, 37, 38, 39, **40**
Antarctica, **8**, 12

Badino, Giovanni, 12, 14
Belize, 30
biologists, 29, **30**
Bruna, Emilio, 41, 42

caves, **10**, 11, **12**, **13**, **14**
Challenger Deep, 35
Challenger (ship), **32**, **38**
conservation, 29, **30**
Curie, Marie, 26–**27**, **38**
Curie, Pierre, 27

Deepsea Challenger (submersible), 35
dropsondes, **23**, 24

earthquakes, 11, 17
ecologists, 41
education, **43**
eye walls, **22**, 23, 24

fangtooth fish, **31**
France, **6**, 26

Hurricane Hunters, **20–21**, 22, **23**, 24
hurricanes, 19, **20–21**, **22–23**, 24

ice caves, **12**

Mariana Trench, 32
meteorologists, 19, 20, **24**

National Hurricane Center (NHC), 21, **24**
Nebraska, **9**
Nobel Prize, 27, 38

oceanographers, 33, 34, 35

Papua, New Guinea, **41**
Poland, 26

radioactivity, 27

samples, **10**, 16, **32**, **35**
scuba diving, **14**, **28**, 30
sharks, **28**, 29, **30**
slurp guns, 35
South Pole, 8, **36**, 37, 38
speleologists, **10**, 11, 12, **13**, **14**
storm chasers, **9**, **25**, 39
Strinati's cave salamanders, **10**
submersibles, **6**, **33**, **34**, **35**

tagging, **30**
telescopes, **36**
timeline, **38–39**
tools, **16**, **21**, **23**, 24, 35
tornadoes, **18**, 19, **25**, 39

underwater caves, **14**

volcanoes, 11, **15–17**, **39**
volcanologists, 11, **15**–17, 39

Weather Reconnaissance Squadron, **20**, **39**
whale sharks, **28**, 29
Woods Hole Oceanographic Institution, **35**

About the Author

Ann O. Squire is a psychologist and an animal behaviorist. Before becoming a writer, she studied the behavior of rats, tropical fish in the Caribbean, and electric fish from central Africa. Her favorite part of being a writer is the chance to learn as much as she can about all sorts of topics. In addition to the Extreme Science books, Dr. Squire has written about many different animals, from lemmings to leopards and cicadas to cheetahs. She lives in Long Island City, New York.